SIGNPOSTS FOR LIVING

A PSYCHOLOGICAL MANUAL FOR BEING

DR KIRSTEN HUNTER

BOOK 1
CONTROL YOUR CONSCIOUSNESS –
IN THE DRIVER'S SEAT

BOOK 2
UNDERSTANDING MYSELF – BE AN EXPERT

BOOK 3
MINDFULNESS AND STATE OF FLOW –
LIVING WITH PURPOSE AND PASSION

BOOK 4
UNDERSTANDING OTHERS –
LOVED ONES TO TRICKY ONES

BOOK 5
PARENTING – LOVE, PRIDE, APPRENTICESHIP

BOOK 6
NAILING BEING AN ADULT – HAVE THE SKILLS

A MEANINGFUL LIFE

DEVOTE YOURSELF TO:

1. **KNOWING** YOURSELF,

2. **LOVING** OTHERS,

3. **LOVING** YOUR COMMUNITY,

4. **GRATITUDE** FOR THE MOMENT, AND

5. **CREATING SOMETHING** THAT GIVES YOU MEANING AND PURPOSE.

First published 2021 by Kirsten Hunter

Produced by Indie Experts P/L, Australasia
indieexperts.com.au

Copyright © Kirsten Hunter 2021

The moral right of the author to be identified as the author of this work has been asserted.

Except for the purposes of reviewing, no part of this publication may be reproduced or transmitted in any form or by any means, electronic or mechanical, including photocopying, recording or any information storage or retrieval system, without the written permission of the author. Infringers of copyright render themselves viable for prosecution.

Cover design and image by Zach Lawry @ Mates Rates Screen Printing & Design
Edited by Jane Smith @ www.janesmitheditor.com
Internal design by Indie Experts
Typeset in URW DIN by Post Pre-press Group, Brisbane

ISBN 978-1-922742-04-9 (paperback)
ISBN 978-1-922742-05-6 (epub)

Disclaimer: Any information in the book is purely the opinion of the author based on personal experience and should not be taken as business or legal advice. All material is provided for educational purposes only. We recommend to always seek the advice of a qualified professional before making any decision regarding personal and business needs.

To Jon

PREFACE TO THE SERIES

This series of books is actually a conversation that I have had with thousands of people over the last twenty years of clinical psychology work. From approximately 42,000 hours of conversations with clients of all shapes and sizes and from all walks of life, all struggling during their various stages in life, I have learnt so much. When you have the same conversation that many times and you see progress, you see where the value lies. I want to share this conversation with you.

'Signpost for Living' is written out of sheer frustration and exhilaration in equal measure. I have limited hours with my clients. This series of books is the information, across the breadth of 'being human' areas, that I would cover with clients if there was no limit to time. This is my 'ideal situation' series, to share with others how to understand and master ourselves. We are pretty dodgy at being human. We really have very little clue about how we work – we don't fully understand our emotions, our behaviour, our neurology, our physiology – or how to live with purpose, calmness, contentment and joy, with our loved ones and within ourselves. This series covers all of these life-challenge hotspots and things we need to learn about ourselves. If we get support, encouragement, and general guidance in these areas, we can get on track quickly. Life can expand and boom us into more contentment and happiness.

How amazing life is if we allow it to be.

If you get a new puppy, it is wise to put in the time to train it; you can enjoy your pup so much more once it's trained. Your pup becomes easy and fun to walk, reliable on your carpets, and an enjoyable character. This is strangely true for *us* too. By studying our thinking, emotions, behaviour and styles of relating to others – really getting a solid level of self-awareness and having a robust skillset – we can enjoy ourselves and our world so much more. And no, we do *not* need to be puppies to learn new tricks; we can learn as adults, at any stage of life. No excuses here. It is absolutely, profoundly, exasperatingly ridiculous that we do not all learn this information routinely at school. 'How to be human, class 101'. Humans have the code to develop physically, but we need more information to develop psychologically into full adults. Not learning these basic life skills can leave us feeling insecure, disconnected and unsafe.

Life is growth. Life is a work in progress.

This is what these books are about. We do not know everything about 'being human' – far from it – but we do know a fair bit. This knowledge, which comes largely through the profession of psychology, is not, however, common knowledge. And yet it should be. It needs to be. We need a manual for being human, for without it we are driving blind.

This series is based on clinical evidence and sound reasoning. It provides clear, calm direction – not all the answers, but solid signposts. Time to share this knowledge with everyone.

WHAT TO EXPECT IN THE 'SIGNPOSTS FOR LIVING' SERIES

The books in the 'Signposts for Living' series are independent but complementary; by strengthening and cultivating one area you enhance all of the other areas simultaneously. There is not much point fixing one hole in the boat when the other holes are not receiving attention. This is not a piecemeal series. We need to cover the whole of human functioning. In this series there will be chapters you need, chapters you don't, chapters that talk to you now, chapters that will tap you on the shoulder in your future. The 'Signposts for Living' series is written for everyone: all ages, mums and dads, grandparents, young adults and teenagers finding their way.

The books are broken down to first explore (in Book 1) how controlling your consciousness can help you grab the reins to your nervous system, thoughts and emotions. Relevant side-alleys that are common traps to dodgy thinking are included. We then flesh out your personal issues in Book 2: *Understanding Myself*. The importance of being awake in life and aware of your present moment is celebrated in Book 3, along with the gem of living with purpose and passion in a state of flow. 'Signposts for Living' then broadens in Book 4 to discuss understanding our relationships with our people (the good, the bad and the ugly). The true complexity of parenting is then dissected in Book 5. Finally, the art of nailing being an adult is fleshed out in Book 6, revealing the excitement of reaping the rewards of becoming a thriving mature human.

To make the books as concise and user-friendly as possible, I have avoided references, footnotes and other scholarly tools as much as possible. The goal is for you to be able to access and use this valuable information without feeling bogged down or needing to have specialised, background knowledge. To acknowledge my sources and guide you to delve deeper, if you wish to, I have included 'further reading' lists where relevant at the end of each book.

Welcome to understanding your humanness.

BOOK 3
MINDFULNESS AND STATE OF FLOW – LIVING WITH PURPOSE AND PASSION

CONTENTS

PART 1: MINDFULNESS

CHAPTER 1	LIVING IN A FOG	3
CHAPTER 2	WHY PRACTISE MINDFULNESS?	8
CHAPTER 3	HOW?	11
CHAPTER 4	WONDERMENT, THROUGH A CHILD'S EYES	15
CHAPTER 5	EXPLORE YOUR PLEASURES	19
CHAPTER 6	AROMAS: MEMORY TRIGGERS	24
CHAPTER 7	LOSS OF INDULGENCE: PACE YOURSELF	26
CHAPTER 8	KITTY LITTER: FIND PLEASURE IN ALL DAILY THINGS	27
CHAPTER 9	MINDFUL EATING VS EATING MINDLESSLY	30
CHAPTER 10	EXPERIENCE THE NOW	38

PART 2: STATE OF FLOW: LIVING WITH PURPOSE AND PASSION

CHAPTER 11	HUMAN BEINGS AT THEIR BEST	41
CHAPTER 12	STATE OF FLOW: LIFE EXPANDING, NOT CONTRACTING	43
CHAPTER 13	WHAT IS YOUR PURPOSE, YOUR PASSION? BUILD YOUR OWN WORLD	53
CHAPTER 14	STATE OF FLOW AT WORK AND STUDY	58
CHAPTER 15	YOUR CREATIVE SELF	62
CHAPTER 16	PROVE SELF TO SELF – MEANING THROUGH HARD WORK	70
CHAPTER 17	YOUR BODY: UNTAPPED RESOURCE FOR STATE OF FLOW	72

CHAPTER 18	SELF-CONTAINED GOALS: DISSOLVE ANXIETY AND BOREDOM	74
IN CONCLUSION		80
FURTHER READING		81
ACKNOWLEDGEMENTS		83
ABOUT THE AUTHOR		85

PART 1
MINDFULNESS

CHAPTER 1
LIVING IN A FOG

Questions for you:

- How did the clouds look this morning? Can you describe them?

- Where is the moon at in its cycle?

- Did you notice the smiling wrinkles around the eyes of the last person you spoke to?

- Thinking about greenery around you, have you noticed the intricate pattern on the leaves?

- Did you stop and taste the individual flavours and textures of your last meal? Could you describe them?

- The smell of the soap you use: how does it come to you in the heat of your shower?

- The last time your loved one smiled at you and hugged you, did you take it in, absorb that moment?

Most of us live in a fog.

We can use mindfulness – awareness of our thoughts, emotions and behaviour – not only to increase our awareness of our problem areas, but also to enable us to enjoy our lives, moment to moment. Let's not be distracted by thinking of the past or future. Not attending to the *now* is like going to the movies with your eyes closed and your ears muffled; you would not enjoy or have a clue about what was going on in the movie.

Think of the movie as your life, scene by scene, what you see in front of you and experience around you. Too often we have our eyes closed. Let's turn our brains on; let's turn our attention on to experiencing our lives. Let's attend to the present moment, which is the only place where life may be fully lived. This here is perhaps the greatest benefit of mindfulness – the skill of living in the here and now: *this moment*.

Living in the moment – suck the marrow.

We rush through our days with such intensity and stress. We grow anxious and worry, magnifying trivia until it becomes important enough to control our lives. The hectic speed of modern life and our constant future-mindedness can become our normal and stop us from living in the present. Technological advances enable us to do more and do it faster. But instead of creating more down time from this efficiency, we have just placed value on squeezing more in.

So, what are we saving time *for*? Our future that we have been looking towards goes by and we don't notice it. We do not stop and live in the now when it comes. What is the point of looking to the horizon if, when we arrive at it, we're just looking out to the next future goal? This culture of 24/7 multitasking and connectivity means that we do not stop in the now to restore our mind and body. We don't realise that *now* holds the moments to remember, to pay attention to; it is *now* that is the most important moment in life.

> *Beware the barrenness of a busy life.*
> Socrates, Greek philosopher

Mindfulness is no small thing. It is enormous. It has enormous ramifications. It is the difference between having a quality life or not. Let's get this really, really clear. *You have only this moment to live.*

Not living in the moment is an irretrievable mistake. First of all, mindfulness begins with becoming aware that we experience *mindlessness* through most of our human activity. We fail to be aware and notice huge swathes of experience. We live and act and react automatically, without much thinking. We need to pay homage to the great Buddhist origins of mindfulness. The Buddhist tradition focuses on achieving a serene state of mind through these practices. These skills of mindfulness are always here, always accessible to you, in each moment.

> We need to cry and laugh less while watching TV, and more while watching real life.

One of the mind's routine habits is to wander into the past and into the future. It's part of the human condition to lose touch with the wonder or mysteries of life in the moment. The mind loses itself in thinking. Pleasant thoughts, painful thoughts, anxious thoughts: this is the monkey mind we spoke about in Book 1. This thinking about past and present monopolises our awareness. These past and present thoughts take over our concentration and take us away from our ability to open our eyes and connect to the present moment. This momentum of *mindlessness* can carry us for decades. We can even go to the grave without knowing that we have only ever actually had *this moment* to live. Why are our eyes closed to our lives? Our life is this moment. Not the future, not the past; *this* moment.

MINDFULNESS. MINDLESSNESS.
We are either mindless about our life this moment,
or we are mindful.
Which makes more sense to you?

You actually have a choice in every moment. You have the choice to be in a wise relationship with this moment, no matter what is happening. Why not be here for each moment? We need to take responsibility for our own experience of the only moment that we have for living, rather than stressing about the past, or brewing on our fears for the future that may never come. We can miss so much if we are consumed with anticipation of our future or rumination about our past.

Understanding this draws us out of our deaf-and-blind automatic pilot mode. This has a profound and transformative impact on how you experience your life. This opens you up to genuine well-being and happiness. The power to do this is innate in all of us. All it takes is paying attention.

Wonder is the beginning of wisdom.
Socrates, Greek philosopher

CHAPTER 2
WHY PRACTISE MINDFULNESS?

Mindfulness is life changing:

1. Mindfulness allows you to cultivate your ability to calm your mind, to relax your body, to concentrate on your moment-to-moment life and to see more clearly.

2. This skill to living helps you feel young at any age. Because you are aware of the many things around you that you can enjoy, it is an embracing approach to your life.

3. You will sleep better.

4. You will become more able to cope with stressful situations.

5. You will feel stronger in your sense of self-worth.

6. Your enthusiasm and enjoyment of work and life will be boosted. Your general sense of contentment will rise from tuning in and enjoying your immediate environment

and experiences, rather than being 'vagued out' or consumed by fear of the future or the past.

7. You will start releasing yourself from social controls. When we plug in to the now and learn to find enjoyment and meaning in this moment, our focus on social pressures melts away. We are no longer looking to outside forces for affirmation.

8. You will benefit from the skill of slowing down the pace of life. This will allow you to make the most of each day and to savour the simple pleasures in life that are all around you in your now.

9. Playfulness is and always will be the ultimate energy generator. Mindfulness is really a playful adventuring within life itself. You will get to engage in the moment-to-moment adventure that life is. This playfulness is one of the best indicators of mental health.

10. Mindfulness allows you to use your best china now, burn your pretty candle now, invite friends over when your house is far from tidy and pristine, and cook intriguing new recipes now. You are enjoying your life now, not saving these special things for a future that continues to move further away as you travel along half asleep. After all, we are not promised tomorrow.

11. Research shows that having appreciation and gratitude are some of the fastest pathways to happiness.

Appreciation is a fundamental and basic outlook on life that can be developed. We need to realise in each moment how lucky we are for what we have.

12. Total involvement in our environment can help us turn our focus away from ourselves. This can be a good antidote to anxiety and depressive mood where we are going in circles thinking about ourselves and our own negative self-talk.

How we meet our life moment by moment is the real meditation practice.

CHAPTER 3
HOW?

When we focus on the now and the world's beauty around us, our bodily sensations dampen the noisy narrative in our heads. Neurologically, we can either be using the brain network that keeps us in the present, or we can be using our analytical brain network. Mindfulness is about consciously turning off all the traffic in our heads, and practising using and strengthening this part of our brain.

Getting into nature has been found to lower rates of mental health issues; getting away from cities and seeking out green spaces gives the pre-frontal cortex of our brain the break that it needs. For example, hiking heightens our sensory reactions to our environment, allowing us to connect more with ourselves and calm ourselves. When we are exposed to awe-inspiring natural experiences, we get a hit of **oxytocin**, the hormone that helps us connect with others and have warm positive feelings. We can clear our heads, and we can make time to quieten our thoughts, to reflect, and create space in our minds. If the hiking is challenging, then we are forced to concentrate on the moment, and our narrative pre-frontal cortex is shushed as we focus on the here and now, and on any present obstacles.

I am fascinated by the world.

Mindfulness doesn't just come about by itself. We have to pay attention, embrace the moment. Nothing more. But given all of our 'doing' and the momentum of life, this 'present moment-ness' seems unusual and may take some effort. It is a new habit of being. To be truly present in the moment means putting aside our anticipations and becoming open to what is happening in the now. We need to tap into our sense of wonder about the world around us.

This is something for *you* to dive into. No one can do it for you. We have to learn how to relate directly to our life. Try to be one hundred percent in the present in one moment, then do the same for the next. It is simply a matter of being present. When you realise that you are not being present, in doing so, you have actually become present. Well done! The moment that you realise your mind is in automatic pilot mode, or you are focusing on the past or the future, you are presented with the choice to come to the present, to look around you at the intricacy of your world: the delicate beauty; the peculiar features of the world around you and your own experience; perhaps your thoughts, your emotions or your bodily sensations. This is mindfulness inviting you to take one moment at a time. We can soon learn how amazing life is if we let ourselves. We can decide to have a beautiful day. We can create our beautiful day by opening our eyes to the beauty and humour of life.

We can learn to suck the marrow out of life. The excitement of travel to a foreign place is a great example of filling our senses. Travelling is such a rich experience as it involves meeting people, touching, sensing, seeing new things – beautiful things, strange things. It's the experience of life. One reason airports can be great is that we find ourselves people-watching there. This is an example of a situation in which we tend to be more in the moment. We have nothing to do, so we sit and watch people; we take in our environment and our world around us. We don't tend to do this in our day-to-day life.

My lovely husband Jon has opened my world to his intriguing country of Basque, Spain. The people of Basque are said to be the original Europeans. Basque has a rich history and eloquent gourmet food; it is wine country and the home of pinchos (tapas), and has lush green rolling mountain countryside that looks like a Tolkien set. I am beyond spoilt. My life experience is so much richer for my Basque experiences. And in turn his is enriched through his experiences of Australia. Travel floods you with new experiences; it expands you and fills you with gratitude.

He who does not travel does not know the value of men.
Moorish Proverb

Many people live for the future. They focus on plans for retirement, and their approach to their money is solely about the future. They do not balance this with quality of life and life adventures now, day by day, in actual lives they are currently living. Many live very conservatively and save for retirement, only to have poor health restrict them when retirement comes, or – for some poor souls – to die prematurely.

They have missed the point. It is about balance. You've got to live and be sensible for the future, but don't live *only* for the future; live for the now. Don't leave the fun stuff for the future; the future may not come. Have fun all along the way. That is your quality of life.

> *Be here. Be present.*
> *Wherever you are, be there.*
> Willie Nelson, singer-songwriter

CHAPTER 4
WONDERMENT, THROUGH A CHILD'S EYES

We need to look at our now with a sense of wonderment, with savouring. This is referred to as 'beginner's mind': the approach of seeing things with curiosity, as new and fresh, as if for the first time. This is a rich experience. Instead of being in our own heads, we are looking through a child's eyes.

We need to not take the ordinary for granted. We need to be awake to all of the extraordinariness around us. *The extraordinariness of the ordinary.* For example, the warmth of water on our skin, the pleasure of clean hands after we have washed them, humour with our less-than-perfect hair from our rushed morning. These thoughts and observations could come just from going to the bathroom at work. This wonderment or beginner's mind then allows us to be open to new possibilities. This fresh approach prevents us from getting stuck in a rut. We stop seeing our day on 'repeat', in 'Groundhog Day' mode. Each moment is unique and contains unique possibilities. For example, when we meet with a familiar person, how open are we to seeing them as if for the first time? How much do we just react to them according to how we have categorised them based on past experiences? Too often we react to our *expectations* of them, not to all of the information that is in front of us.

Savouring is the deliberate awareness of and attention to a pleasure. It is a conscious experiencing of a pleasure that allows you to enjoy the moment as if you don't want it to end.

Here are some ways to boost our savouring and wonderment in the moment:

1. Be everywhere you are. Sharpen your senses. I often say to our kids, 'Look with your eyes.' It sounds silly but it means, '*Really* look; look so that you could describe with detail once you have looked away. Study the beauty, the intricacy, the peculiarity of what you can see in front of you, what you can taste, what you can feel with your bodily sensations; listen to the different elements of the music, connect with the feelings it stirs in you, good or bad. Luxuriate and indulge in your senses.'

2. Self-talk when you are impressed by yourself or others, or aware of how long you have waited for this experience to happen. Realise how momentous an experience is in the moment, not just later. Be conscious of your own praise and congratulations.

3. Share your experience with others, talking through the experience *while* you are both experiencing it.

4. Try to have a break from thinking, and just *sense*. Absorb. We often only see our surrounding environment through a veil of our own thoughts and opinions. Try now to see the trees, the sky, the stars and the leaves with an uncluttered mind. Don't be in critical analysis mode; be more like a visitor to that moment, open to noticing the details. We want to lose ourselves in the wonder of the moment.

5. Consciously think about taking mental photographs as your experience happens. Or taking a souvenir of the event (not an illegal piece of history or nature of course!) so that you can remember the experience later.

6. Consciously work to make your stale experiences in life fresh. Express your approach to each moment with gratitude, rather than taking life for granted.

7. Because we live so unconsciously, we take the skills of our body for granted. We don't appreciate the balance and strength of walking until we cannot walk, we do not appreciate the dexterity of our fingers and hand grip until we have this taken from us for some reason. The truth is these skills and abilities are miracles.

8. Hug other people well and have regular massages. We humans tend to lose our physical connections with others. Make it a priority. Savour touch.

9. Explore your pleasures. See below...

Nothing is worth more than this day.
Johann Wolfgang von Goethe, poet

CHAPTER 5
EXPLORE YOUR PLEASURES

Pleasures are 'raw feels'. They are clear sensations that allow positive strong emotions. They last for a moment. They are delightful sights and sounds, delicious tastes and smells, sexual feelings, personal feelings and the feeling of your body moving well. They involve little thinking, just *noticing*. From these pleasures we can feel comfort, ecstasy, thrill, amusement, relaxation, rapture, fun, bliss ... By simply observing, we open ourselves up and allow for expansion, because we begin to explore the world beyond our sleepwalking usual routines. We can place ourselves outside our usual comfort zones. This creates zest for life.

Let's break it down:

TOUCH

The warmth from a fire
Stroking of gentle touch
Hugging the people you love
When you are covered in dirt and grime,
the feeling of a hot shower to wash it away
Sensual touch
Orgasm, say no more
The strength of massage
Sculpture that you yearn to touch
Fabrics that you have to run through your fingers
Having your hair washed by someone
Fresh linen, hot towels
A meaningful hug.

SIGHTS

Become an observer of beauty;
this allows us to delight in the world
Clouds, or a crisp expansive blue sky
Waves rolling, crashing in
Photos, images that make your heart sing
The beauty of interactions of animals, a pigeon's dance,
the depth you see in a horse's eye,
birds flying in formation
The faces of children playing, their absorption in their
enthusiasm, living their dream state
The dance of flames on the fire
Artwork that enchants you, touches you. We live in a time
where with a touch of a button all of the artworks in all of
the world's galleries are available

People-watching, looking at the faces of people, not their material shell. Looking for their uniqueness; everyone has beauty in their individuality. How boring if we were all cardboard cut-outs of the same creature type
The bizarre in nature; a crazy-shaped tree. Have you ever noticed a goat's pupil?
Taking a drive through a picturesque landscape.

SOUNDS

Music, the universal language, that fills you with exuberance, that resonates deep within you
Feeling harmonies and joy pulse through you
The sound of laughter
Singing: it is intoxicating; you lose yourself
Listening to rain
Listening to animals, the intelligence of whales.

TASTES

Great food
New foods
Comforting food that speaks to you of home
Curious food
Beautiful wine
Eating slowly
Noticing the interplay of tastes on your tongue
Eating at a table, away from the distraction of technology and work
One bite at a time
Putting down cutlery between bites. Trying chopsticks
Using nice plates and glasses so that you savour.

SMELLS

The crisp smell of a forest
Tree, flower and herb aroma; sandalwood, ginger, cinnamon, nutmeg, eucalyptus, cedar, rose, lemon
The welcoming smell of a bakery
The salty air of the ocean
Freshly cut grass
Summer rain in the air
A baby's head
Perfume
The smell of delicious food cooking
Aromas play a vital role in our enjoyment of food,
75% of our flavour in taste comes from first smelling our food or drink,
our taste buds twitch, we salivate with anticipation
We choose who we are attracted to based on their smell
There is a strong association between aromas and our mood.

MOVEMENT

Yawning release, so good
Fluent movement of the body
Feelings of strength and coordination in your limbs
Using your body to achieve things
Dance, be a child again, release, feel the rhythm. Let it touch you and move you, your body moves on its own
Laughing so hard your sides hurt.

EMOTIONAL EXPERIENCES

A special glance
Falling in love
The miracle of your child, every day
Watching your sports team win
Making new friends or spending time with old ones
Hearing appreciation
The sense of adventure and travelling to new places
Discovering a new idea
Discovering that love is more powerful than time
Watching the expression on someone's face when they open a heart-felt gift from you
The smiles of our special people
A really great story
Staying in love.

These are the treasures of life.

CHAPTER 6
AROMAS: MEMORY TRIGGERS

I am going to make a special mention about the power of our sense of smell. The olfactory nerve is responsible for your sense of smell. It links directly to the hippocampus in your brain where your memories are stored. This is why certain smells can remind us so strongly and so instinctively of long-forgotten memories. It's life enhancing to be aware of this and to pay curious attention to this hidden doorway to our past.

I walked into my kitchen last week. I unfortunately smelt a strange unpleasant odour: the smell of old fat on a pan that had not been washed properly. Boom! I was nine years old again when I knew an elderly, humble man called Lofty from Cunnamulla, in outback Australia. An appropriate name for this towering man. My taste buds were triggered to contemplate the mint slice biscuits that he always offered. I don't remember the conversations we had, but I remember that he was always interesting. And I remember that he was generous in sharing his very impoverished supplies that even as a child I did not want to take from him. My memory has me recalling a sense of the man, and a sense of his dwelling. A gentle giant, who was loving and perhaps lonely, who had lived a very simple life. Spending time with him extended my world. I'm taken back there, all from a smell triggering my memory.

CHAPTER 7
LOSS OF INDULGENCE: PACE YOURSELF

Pleasures play a crucial part in living fully. We cannot, however, build our life purely around these pleasures because they are momentary, and because we become accustomed to them.

This process of becoming accustomed to pleasures is called **habituation**. When we are habituated, we require difference and novelty, or bigger doses of the experience to get the same original amount of pleasure. Rapidly indulging in the same pleasures diminishes the pleasure received. Pleasures are about enjoyment, not psychological growth; they do not provide the complexity of satisfaction that comes from meaningful pursuits.

The answer is to enjoy – to luxuriate in the pleasures, all of them, all around you – but to space out the pleasures to keep them rich in freshness. You can have too much of a good thing. How we spread and space out pleasures over time is crucial. The first thirty minutes in an art gallery is far more enjoyable then the last thirty minutes of your visit. We need to be aware of the freshness of our absorption and pace ourselves. Don't overdo it.

CHAPTER 8
KITTY LITTER: FIND PLEASURE IN ALL DAILY THINGS

Mindfulness is about awareness in the moment, and naturally works with pleasurable experiences. But what about the neutral events that we routinely have to do? What about unpleasurables? Things that are just a bit nasty in life (like smelly nappies and kitty litter)? Then there is the very long list of daily mundane chores and obligations. This might be a hard thing to sell, but if you find positive meaning in what you are doing, you can find satisfaction and even pleasure in even the undesirable things. This is core to controlling your consciousness and being mindful and awake in the moment. There is no room for autopilot with the undesirable things in life.

So here we go. What do you enjoy about cleaning kitty litter? I enjoy having it all clean at the end and having all smells gone (even for a little while). So when I go to clean the kitty litter, I mindfully enjoy that I am getting it clean. This is where my focus and experience goes to. When you go to a sink full of dishes, you will enjoy having it all cleaned away, so you focus on and take pleasure in the process of doing that. You can also enjoy the warmth of the water on your hands and the short break from your higher-order head work. When you are searching and searching for a car park, you can appreciate that with time you will be able to park and go about your outing. You can relax with the process and enjoy the achievement when you eventually find a park. When you go outside to hang out clothes, you can decide to take pleasure in shaking out and creating your systems with the clothes as you peg them out. You can enjoy the weather – either the sunshine or, if it is cool, you can enjoy the knowledge that you will soon have a warm house to return to. We need to make our approach to our mundane chores intrinsically rewarding. Otherwise we are doing them out of reluctant obligation.

I realise that this sounds very 'happy-happy', but this is not about being falsely optimistic and looking on the bright side. This is about being completely practical. You can go to a task and focus on the obvious negative and mundane side to it and feel displeasure in the grind of life. Or you can look at the other component that is factually accurate and, through that focused attention, you can genuinely derive pleasure from these same events. Automatic pilot brings you a negative and mundane experience. Controlling your consciousness and being mindful in the moment of the positive experience involved will give you pleasure and satisfaction. It actually re-energises you. It is your choice.

Another extremely important skill is to apply this to daily involvement with family. We easily become complacent and take family for granted when we see them all the time. It is therefore essential that we learn to be awake in the moment with our family. Be mindful of your precious time with them. To prioritise their company, to stop being busy, and *be* with them. We need to savour our time with our children, spouses, parents (and co-workers and friends) as richly and with as much enjoyment as possible. Don't have regrets for not appreciating time with them. Make relationships your priority. Keep them as healthy as possible.

People often ask me, how do I have five boys, run a bursting private psychology practice, run the business side of things, have quality time with my beautiful Jon, and be fairly consistently buoyant with energy? Using this skill is a huge percentage of the answer. I refuel from the mundane. I enjoy the mundane. I can do it through mindfulness in the moment and creative foresight – by asking myself, 'What can I find pleasure and satisfaction in here?' Try it.

CHAPTER 9
MINDFUL EATING VS EATING MINDLESSLY

DO YOU NOTICE EATING?

Most people's minds are often somewhere else when they are eating. Perhaps we work through our lunch 'break', perhaps we watch something, or get engrossed in conversation, or flick through social media, or read or just zone out. We often hardly notice the food that we are placing in our mouths and eating. It is one of the great pleasures in life and we are asleep to it. We miss out on enjoying the food we have just made, or paid for, and we are far more likely to overeat.

Maybe this is another reason why expensive food is usually more delicious? We actually stop to taste it and to explore it because we are paying a lot for it. If it was cheap, we might just put it in our mouths mindlessly and not notice its flavour as much. We can definitely become complacent with home-cooked food that is routinely prepared for us, and we can be surprised when a guest remarks on the flavour of our home eats. It is novel to them and they are paying attention to tastes that we have been spoilt with daily. More gratitude is needed.

CHEW, CHEW, CHEW

Chewing is the first stage of our digestion, but do we chew effectively? For most of us the answer is no. Take smaller bites and chew, chew, chew. When we eat mindlessly, we often almost inhale our food; we take big bites and we don't chew enough. But often if we slow down, intentionally taking smaller bites, chewing adequately, we can reduce or even eliminate digestion problems.

ARE YOU HUNGRY?

It is a skill to be aware of our bodies and notice whether we are truly hungry or not. We need to learn to be aware of when we've had enough to eat and it's time to stop. If we are looking for a boost of energy or a change to our mood, we need to think through and investigate what is going on. Are we reaching for a sugar energy hit or comfort carbs? Do we need more sleep? Do we need to take more windows out of our fast pace to recharge? Are we stressed, and can we address our stress? Are we actually eating because we are hungry or for one of these other reasons? Reaching for food as a quick fix is a patch-up solution that's going to last for only a very short time; then we are back to square one again.

EMOTIONAL EATING EQUALS ZONING OUT

We need to be aware of when we eat for emotional reasons. The coping mechanism of soothing or dulling our emotions with food does not address the problem. The emotional problems will just return. Also, we are likely to regret our mindless consumption, as excessive eating is obviously not good for our health. We need to bring mindful self-inquiry to our emotions. What is going on? Let's write down how we are feeling and thinking. Let's start working to process and address the problem areas.

The reason emotional eating works in the short term is that when we put food in our mouths we tend to zone out. We usually only taste the first mouthful, and then as long as we can keep shovelling food into our mouths we can disconnect from our negative thoughts and emotions. It is the same 'disappearing' that we do with shopping, gambling, drinking, smoking, drugs; we are self-medicating.

We can also learn **comfort eating** as a coping mechanism from our childhood. As a child when you were sick or unhappy, family may have offered you comfort food. Now as an adult, comfort food may be your go-to when you are feeling sad or anxious. What are your patterns? When do you comfort eat? Over what kind of stressors? What are your go-to comfort foods? What patterns can you look out for so that you can make a conscious choice in the future?

We can learn to act when our uncomfortable emotions trigger our urge to eat mindlessly and unhealthfully. Remember, in the moment you can choose your response. How you respond will shape your relationship with food and your body.

WHICH FOOD FITS YOU?

It is amazing how unaware we can be of food we eat. We need to be mindful of which foods we choose to eat so that we can enjoy food and take care of ourselves. We often carry on with bad habits; we feel bad from the foods we've eaten but continue to eat them on repeat, mindlessly.

Have you worked out your unique relationship with food and what actually works for you? Do you feel better or worse, for example, if you eat gluten or lactose? How do carbohydrates work for you? What is your relationship with sugar? How much protein feels best? What is a good pacing of meals for you? Regular and small meals, or three main meals, or two main meals? Experimenting with your body and experimenting with your food require mindful attention to your body. It is worth putting in the time to research your best formula; then you are set. The goal is usually to feel light in your digestion. The goal is to eat the right amount and the right type of food that will give you energy without leaving you bloated and stodgy.

Our family often jokes that we only eat 'sexy food'. But this is actually true; we eat food that is exciting in its quality, simplicity, nutritional value and care in being prepared. Simple is fine. Simple food is often in itself a beautiful thing, as long as it is of good quality and has mixed colours and lovely flavour. We need to slow down our relationship with food so that we have intent and enjoyment.

THE FAMOUS MINDFUL EATING EXPERIMENT

This is strange but interesting to do. This is an experiment in truly being mindful with a mouthful of food. All you need is one fresh sultana and curiosity.

Take a sultana. First, take the time to smell it. How would you describe the smell – does it conjure up emotions, memories or associations? Put the sultana on your lips. What do your lips tell you about its texture? Put the sultana in your mouth without biting it, and roll it around in your mouth. What does your tongue notice? What is the flavour like? Take your time. Now intentionally bite into the sultana. Has the flavour changed? Intensified? Does this flavour conjure up emotions, memories or associations? If you needed to describe a sultana to someone who has never encountered one, how would you describe the smell, texture and taste of the simple yet strangely complex sultana?

We are not going to go through our days regularly mindfully eating sultanas. This experiment is to learn the slowing down and intentional studying pace of mindful eating. If you transfer even a quarter of these mindful eating skills to your day-to-day eating, then you are miles ahead. You will enjoy your food, only eat quality food, and only eat when you intend to and are hungry.

Food is fuel. You would not put dodgy fuel in your car because then your car would not run. It's the same with your body.

TRICKS TO STAY AWAKE TO MINDFUL EATING

1. Before you eat, take a moment to notice what is going on for you. Are you feeling stressed or relaxed? What is your mood? What are you thinking? Are you feeling anxious, sad or irritated? What is eating doing for you right now? Do you *need* food or are you simply escaping from your problems?

2. Always sit down. Don't eat on the go. This helps us appreciate our food.

3. Take away distractions while eating. Eating is a conversation between you and your food. Attend to it. Have a rule: no working while eating. Take yourself away from your usual workspace to eat. No screens while eating. Just take a moment out for yourself to notice and enjoy eating.

4. When possible, eat with nice plates and glasses. They do not cost much, and they enhance the meal. Especially don't eat mindlessly out of a bag.

5. Serve out portions that would fit on a bread-and-butter plate. That is plenty. Even serve it on this smaller plate if you choose. This also helps you to know what you are eating. It takes away the 'finish everything on your plate' problem, as you won't have as much on your plate to begin with. And no, to make the point, we do *not* have to finish everything on our plate; the negative impact on our bodies of overeating is more important than the problem of seeing food wasted.

6. Try to slow down your eating by cutting your food up more, eating with cutlery when you normally might not. Even eat more with chopsticks if that works for you. Put down your cutlery between bites or at regular intervals.

7. Notice how your stomach is feeling, then rest for a bit and let the food reach your stomach. Your stomach may literally be so stretched that it has become desensitised to the sensation of fullness. It might take some time of more moderate-sized meals for your stomach to recover and start functioning so that it can gauge its fullness.

8. While eating, have gratitude for the meal; think about and appreciate where the ingredients came from

and the long chain of people who have prepared it for you (the seed company, the farmers, the pickers, the packagers, the finance people, the marketers, the transporters, the shop managers, shop workers and all of the family members who supported these people to go do their work roles). All for the food on your plate. Have gratitude that you have the food, the moment to eat, and the surroundings around you.

CHAPTER 10
EXPERIENCE THE NOW

You have a choice. You can stay in the world amongst those who have their eyes and ears closed and their touch, taste and smell dampened. You can remain half awake. The richness and joy that is in front of and around you can pass you by. You can continue to live for tomorrow, or remain swimming in the past. Or you can open your eyes, your ears and your mind to your life – the one that you are actually living in this here moment. This being the only life that you have: the *present*. And you can look for the beauty, the joy, the humour and the sentiment that is almost always in reach. You can feel that goofy smile and appreciation that this level of mindfulness naturally brings.

Please wake up and stay awake. Experience the now. Please don't sleep through the movie that is your life.

PART 2
STATE OF FLOW: LIVING WITH PURPOSE AND PASSION

CHAPTER 11
HUMAN BEINGS AT THEIR BEST

Perhaps the most fundamental human needs are personal freedom and a sense of meaning in our existence and the world that we are part of. We talk about being authentic, living an authentic life. This means that we are simply being ourselves. We are not imitating what we think we 'should' be or what we are told we 'should' do. We are living in a way that enables our actions and words to be consistent with our beliefs and values.

We are not, however, very good at doing this. In fact, if we look around, most of us are living as puppets, with superficial pressures and pressures from other people and our own insecurity holding the strings. This chapter is about a vital ingredient in waking up and living fully.

Living fully means movement and growth, not arrival at some point in our lives and then stagnantly sitting still. Life is not about the *destination* that we aim to arrive at; it is the constant *process* of getting there. Happiness comes from the learning process and effort. I spent eleven years at university, and while there I thought the whole point was graduating and getting my clinical Ph.D. It wasn't. What mattered, and what it was actually about, was my learning – day to day, clinically, and through life experience. This is what gave me meaning and is what I have used in the following chapters of my life, not the pieces of paper stating my qualifications (though they were very helpful!).

The key to so many life pursuits is not to hurry the journey of life. It is better if the journey lasts for years, so you are old by the time you arrive, wealthy with all you have gained on the way, wise – as you will have become – and so full of experience.

Despite the pressure of messages that we receive from popular Western culture today, you do *not* need material things or physical beauty to reach for a fulfilled life. Aristotle nailed this long ago when he argued that the thriving way of life comes from moral and psychological excellence, not material possession or physical attributes. He believed that happiness required the fulfilment of human potentialities. This golden truth goes back further to Aristotle's teacher, Plato. And *his* teacher, Socrates. Socrates famously said, 'We cannot live better than in seeking to become better.' The ancient Greek also spoke of 'human' work through which you make a courageous difference. We need to live towards reaching our potential in most things.

CHAPTER 12
STATE OF FLOW: LIFE EXPANDING, NOT CONTRACTING

At some point in life, hopefully, we learn that we are happiest and healthiest when our lives are expanding rather than contracting. We feel a purpose in living when we feel a connection to something. If we're unable to express our true character we feel empty and inauthentic. Without growth we feel depressed, and with age it starts to gnaw on us – this realisation that we are fidgeting until we die.

The gnawing realisation that we are fidgeting until we die.

Enter **Csikszentmihalyi!**

The Hungarian-American psychologist Mihaly Csikszentmihalyi (pronounced 'Me-high Cheeks-sent-me-high') investigated and named the concept of **'state of flow'**. His legacy is the study of what is key to thriving and living optimally. You reach state of flow when you feel as if you are doing exactly what you want to be doing – you never want it to end, and you feel as if time has stopped. It is passion and purpose. Let's explain.

A state of flow is the state that you experience when you do things that give you meaning and purpose – that are challenging enough to extend you, but not so challenging that they stress you. We feel content in our being when our body or mind is stretched to its limits in a voluntary effort to accomplish something that we feel is worthwhile. We feel it when we're making our optimal experience happen.

For a child, it could be creating a structure out of cardboard that is alive with their imagination. For someone starting to incorporate exercise into their lives it could be being able to walk or run the distance with a sense of increased capability and fitness. For a pianist, it could be working to finally master a challenging composition. For all of us there are thousands upon thousands of avenues we can take to extend ourselves in meaningful pursuits, and to live through a state of flow. Singing, enjoying a great conversation, reading a good book, kayaking, dancing, kicking a goal, are all examples of activities that can make time stop. If our skills match the challenge, we are in touch with our capabilities.

Flow activities involve a sense of discovery and push us to a higher level of performance. We are living to our ambition. We are growing ourselves by making our experiences and skills more complex and advanced. The key to flow activities is this growth of the self.

A state of flow can also be experienced during times of great stress and adversity. For example, parents waiting in hospital with a sick child can relish in achieving the tasks that they can do to organise their situation. They can busy themselves with new meaningful challenges like learning about the hospital processes, the medication regimes, and their ability to meet their child's unique needs. Human capacity is inspiring. The great news is that state of flow is open to all of us, no matter the circumstances. It is a mind skill and it has nothing to do with outside resources.

Finding the balance between matching your skills with the complexity of the task is vital. If the challenge is beyond your skill level you will become stressed, and this is unpleasant and punishing. If the challenge is too far below your abilities, then you will become bored and you will watch the clock ticking.

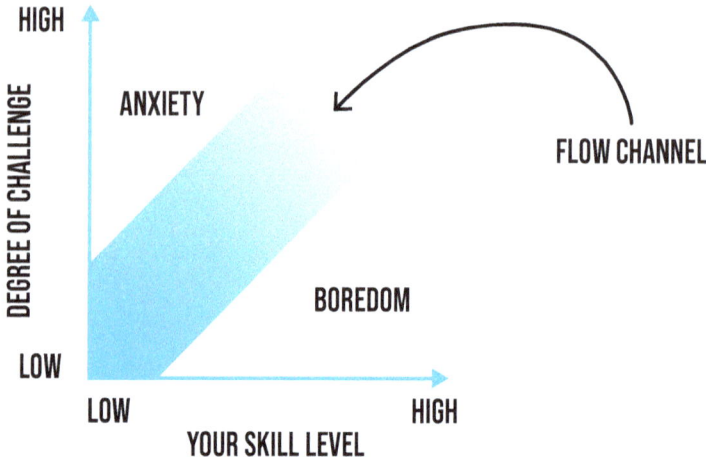

Flow makes it possible to achieve happiness through control over one's inner life. We cannot enjoy doing the same thing that demands the same level of competency for long. We need growth and discovery. To enjoy a state of flow, our energy and attention need to be invested in realistic goals, with our skills matching the opportunities for action. If the task is too repetitively easy, we either grow bored or frustrated. Our desire to enjoy ourselves again pushes us to discover new opportunities and to stretch our skills. When we are in this state of flow we concentrate; we have deep, effortless involvement. We have clear goals and we have a sense of control. By the way, this does not mean you need to go out and quit your job if it has become mundane. The key is to make it *not* mundane. I will explain.

Live in the here and now.

What is really interesting is that when we are so immersed in our state of flow, *our sense of our self vanishes* and time seems to stop. We can look up from our task and time seems to have disappeared. We have also had a break from self-reflection. We are not thinking about ourselves, which is a rare thing.

While this is a very positive experience, another fascinating feature is that the state of flow is actually without emotion. While we will afterwards reflect with a deep sense of enjoyment and satisfaction that may be long cherished – this state of flow can even become a landmark in memory, an example of what life should be like – when we are actually in the state of flow there is an *absence of emotion*. We are completely *in the zone of concentration*. We don't need conscious awareness of emotion (which has the usual function of warning us) because we are doing exactly what we feel we should be doing at that moment.

Because we must allocate attention to our task at hand, we momentarily forget everything else. This is *the optimal state of inner experience*. This brings order to our consciousness. It is these periods of striving and struggling to overcome our challenges that we find to be the most enjoyable times of our lives. We are growing into a more complex version of ourselves. We are stretching our skill and reaching for higher challenges; we are becoming more extraordinary.

Flow occurs when the challenges you face *match* and then *extend* your abilities to meet them. These moments are not relaxing or passive times. They are actually created when we dedicate and apply ourselves. To not become overwhelmed by a task, we need to choose realistic challenges that we can master largely on our own. We need to transform daunting, vague goals into feasible goals. Defining our goals is a crucial ingredient. It is then that we can experience flow and feel a sense of pride and self-esteem.

Here is another slightly bizarre twist. When we are in a state of flow, it might not necessarily feel pleasant at the time. The runner's legs may feel at fever pitch of pain as they run the last lap. The entrepreneur may be faced with a long list of unknowns and hurdles, and few resources – and yet they will reflect later with deep satisfaction on these moments, and prize the memories.

When people engage in these more ambitious pursuits, they must put in a lot of effort to control their consciousness, and it can be painful. But they are pursuing a sense of mastery. They are actively shaping their lives and moving forward. They are pushing themselves to live into and beyond what they had imagined to be achievable. Afterwards, they know they have changed, that they have grown, and that they have become more complex. The experience is so enjoyable that they will do it even at great cost, purely for the sake of doing it; nothing else seems to matter.

Take my writing of this book, for example. I've been writing it for fifteen months now and I'm up to the point of sending it to an editor soon. I have put enormous numbers of hours into this and had to be very creative, determined and self-disciplined to make time around my many other full-time pursuits to write it. But the sense of satisfaction that I feel is significant and I have been spending most of the writing time in a state of flow. I flew back from Basque and barely noticed the twenty-seven-hour trip because when I wasn't sleeping, I was immersed in writing. Time disappeared, and before I knew it I was back in Australia. This was a surreal flight, time wise!

Being in the moment (as when we're practising mindfulness) and being in a state of flow are two optimal but very different experiences. When you are in the moment you are in time and you're fully *aware*, while in a state of flow you 'disappear' from time and you are immersed in *doing*. When we are in the moment, we experience an immediate pleasure and a sense of captivation and appreciation. While in a state of flow we strangely have an absence of emotion, but afterwards will report it as very positive. Think of being in the moment and state of flow as being in two different gears: both bring us contentment and true joy. We cannot base our lives on purely focusing on pleasures in the moment. We cannot rely on the them purely as attempted shortcuts to living well. This does not work. When we live for pleasures, meaning and authenticity are nowhere to be found. This is why we must also experience a state of flow regularly in our daily life pursuits to ground us and form a basis for a meaningful life.

When someone is in a state of flow they do not feel self-consciousness. Self-consciousness is our most common form of distraction and often trips us up. State of flow allows us not to worry about how we are doing or how we look from the outside; rather we are completely consumed and committed to our goals. This is a continued complementary dance because when we lack self-consciousness, deeper involvement is possible. But also, our depth of involvement allows us to push any self-consciousness away – and so the cycle continues.

There is another intriguing dance in the state of flow. If we pay attention to our immersed flow *experience* instead of worrying about *ourselves*, we no longer feel like a separate individual; paradoxically, we feel stronger. We grow beyond the limits of our individuality by investing in the interaction and the system, rather than ourselves. This allows our *self* to emerge with a higher level of complexity. We can rise above our own insecurities and concerns about ourselves.

TEENS AND STATE OF FLOW

Let's look at the contrast between groups of people who have frequent states of flow and those who experience them rarely, if at all. Sadly, contrasting groups of teenagers provide a perfect example of how state of flow affects well-being. Let's call them 'low-flow' and 'high-flow' teen groups.

Low-flow groups live on gaming and watching screens, and if they venture out, it will be to hang out in each other's homes on even more technology, or at shopping malls. The high-flow teens have sports and hobbies, and they spend time on schoolwork or casual jobs. The high-flow teens are found to have healthier psychological well-being but believe the low-flow teens are having more fun. While they may be reluctant about their high-flow life, their approach to life pays off later. The high-flow teens go on to have better engagement in education, deeper social connections, and more positive career outcomes. They are investing in an approach to living that sets them up with good habits for life.

STATE OF FLOW PARENTING

Parenting is perhaps one of our most meaningful roles in life, and state of flow is at play here also. Parents enjoy the unfolding of their babies' and children's growth. They wait in anticipation to celebrate the first smiles, the first words, the growing ability to reach for things, crawl, stand, walk, read, write, tie shoelaces, negotiate friendships, follow a class routine. Parents keep guiding and supporting their children towards the next challenge, helping them to learn to match their skills to their new adventures into the world.

This does not stop at childhood, however, and it is vital that parents do not then leave their teenagers to their own devices. Teenagers are actually at the 'life apprentice' stage; this is the most crucial time for them to extend themselves into early adulthood. This might be through household skills and financial accountability, having a positive approach to learning and pride in work, and learning to pursue and dedicate themselves to interests and sports.

Unfortunately, many parents step away at this crucial stage. They see their teenager's non-receptive attitude and take a lead from it. They perhaps don't have the relationship foundation to ask their teenager to do things they don't want to do but that will be good for them. But it is at this stage that we develop crucial habits of involvement in life.

CHAPTER 13
WHAT IS YOUR PURPOSE, YOUR PASSION? BUILD YOUR OWN WORLD

When we are experimenting and expanding who we are, we need to look around for areas that intrigue us and notice which parts of life's playground we want to play on. This personalised approach is a crucial ingredient in our state of flow, as we need to find areas to explore and engage in that match our level of skills. We need to be curious and interested in the world. Life is an adventure. We need to learn to live well with others and learn to be ourselves. When we learn, we have gone from not knowing something to knowing something, and that is exciting. The creation of knowledge is a great satisfaction.

What makes you come alive?

We need to be like a bower bird, continuing to collect and further develop new passions. 'Passionate' is not a word that we use enough. There is so much joy in discovering new ideas, skills and ways of viewing life. Build your *own* world, not someone else's – a world that is unique to you. This is about continuing to know yourself; it's a journey that fortunately never ends. We need to be like a moving stream, not a stagnant pool. Our unique interests and experiences and how we express them give us the individuality and authenticity that we celebrate. If you find that you really want to achieve something – something that draws great passion and purpose – you will find a way.

Hobbies regenerate you. They are something creative just for you. You do them for the pleasure and satisfaction; they make you happy. You don't do them for money. There's no pressure, no expectations. Hobbies *give* to you; they do not take away. What does engaging in hobbies look like? We could explore a passion for discussing current events, new ideas, meaningful projects, and the excitement of future developments. Or we can devour new skills, new adventures, crafts, arts, music, dancing, books, films, painting, poems, conversations, the study of nature, architecture. Or find an angle of meaning in sport that makes sense to us: to socialise and relax, or to refine our skills or boost our health. Whatever the mix of passions and hobbies you choose and keep choosing, what matters is that they speak directly to your soul.

*Passion is powerful. Nothing was ever achieved without it and nothing can take its place. No matter what you face in life, if your passion is great enough, you will find the strength to succeed. Without passion life has no meaning. So, put your heart, mind and soul into even your smallest acts. This is the essence of passion.
This is the secret to life.*
Anonymous

We don't need to choose between our passions. It is important in fact *not* to pick and choose between them, so that you can bounce between them. When you tire of one project or interest you can move to another. This will keep your interest fresh, and you can work with what you are drawn to. So keep *all* of your passions in your life; don't throw any of yourself away. Become a leader in your personal life. Don't wait for others to create your interests and possibilities. This is a quiet and personal conversation for yourself.

Do you need money? No, not with regard to leisure. Research has found that leisure activities that are expensive and require outside resources (such as driving or power boating or technology-based activities) provide less enjoyment and state of happiness than inexpensive leisure activities. We are happiest with the simpler things in life: hobbies, engaging conversations, reading, gardening, craft, building – all of which require high investment from our attention and involvement. It is not about new toys that we own, it is about what we do with our hands and our brains. It is self-driven. When you engage in leisure activities that rely on external resources, less creativity is required and you will therefore experience less enjoyment and fewer memorable rewards.

Our passions are really about creating our own worlds, our own culture. We need our lives to overflow with our passions. It is about growth, expansion of yourself and your world. The more life experience you have, the richer you become. We need to live our life so that it counts. Life is a time of great energy, enterprise and endeavour. I wish you much joy in your search for what lights you up – your passions.

Often living true to ourselves means taking creative risks. We need to foster a sense of daring, to have a go. This means expanding our ambitions and broadening our normal horizons. So many people who get a big shock with a scary health diagnosis realise that they have been treading water, putting off their aspirations and playing life safe. They realise that they've allowed their life to become a monotonous routine, and they're bored by it. Life is about not wasting time; it is about absorbing interesting and meaningful pursuits and truly challenging yourself. If we are not regularly outside of our comfort zone, we are not expanding.

So be an interesting person by living an interesting life. If you have a tendency to do nothing and to remain unchanged, then you are living a life of inertia. You are not living; you are sitting on your hands. Where there is inertia there is no creativity, and there is no living well. Your life is precious; *you* are precious. Have high standards for your life. This does not necessarily mean travel to all of the world's continents or set up a large business. This means do those things that are important to you. They may be quiet acts of learning or creativity, reaching out to loved ones or loved causes, challenging your skillset, scratching an itch. Whether it is learning the guitar, finally having that overseas trip, writing a play or landscaping your garden, get busy with it. Wake up planning or scheming with enthusiasm to get into it.

CHAPTER 14
STATE OF FLOW AT WORK AND STUDY

It is easy to understand the state of flow in areas of creativity, sport and hobbies. We choose them in the first place to make us happy. But we cannot just rely on leisure in our pursuit of contentment. We spend a large majority of our waking time at work and study, and this area of life is an ideal time for state of flow. Work and study usually have clear rules of performance and clear goals. Hopefully we receive feedback about whether we are on track and performing well or not. Concentration is usually valued, and we minimise distractions. If work matches our challenges to our skills, we can feel a state of flow at work; when we immerse ourselves, time disappears and we come out feeling satisfaction and contentment. We may not feel the exhilaration of climbing a high peak on a daily basis, but nevertheless we are in that optimal state of flow channel.

When we study, if we can approach our learning with a desire to grow and extend, rather than just aim to get another piece of assessment done, then we will facilitate more frequent states of flow. We will create more meaning and relate to our studies with purpose. This will immediately increase our concentration, and therefore our skill, and the state of flow channel rewards us. The alternative is being dragged through study in a state of pressure or boredom, which is of course very negative. What happens when we are in a negative headspace? We procrastinate more and concentrate less; this, sadly, is the approach of most of the population. It's time to break through and get this right. A desire to grow and extend is the simple answer.

What is the meaning of life? To be happy and useful.
His Holiness the Dalai Lama

What if we don't love our work from the outset? Of course there are the workplaces that are detrimental to us; perhaps there is a toxic culture, or we feel unsafe with our colleagues or the work environment is seriously an ill fit. If so, of course, be as proactive as you can to find an alternative workplace. You spend an enormous part of your life at work, so it's pretty appalling if it is a harmful place for you.

But what of the adequate workplaces that just don't routinely challenge and push us? It is true that if you view work as pure drudgery, this experience and outlook can bury you. We need to be aware, however, that it can be easier to complain about our dull or stressed work life than to re-invent ourselves. Our jobs don't need to be extraordinary; the key is that we can recraft our mundane jobs to increase our enjoyment and frequency of state of flow. This means finding a new approach to work. We need to look for genuine meaning and avenues to extend our strengths of character in our work role so that we hit the zone of state of flow more often.

Perhaps our role is part of the bigger system and we don't get to see a direct outcome from our work. We may feel like a gear in the machine. But without each gear, the machine does not work. We need to remodel our perception and approach to work daily, so that we can find value in the impact of the role that we play. We find purpose when we are working for the greater good.

Consider, for example, an accountant who sees that their awareness and processing of figures creates the foundations for a business to function. In seeing that there is a direct ripple effect to the community, they see value in the role. The accountant also values that their financial management helps small-business mums and dads keep their family financially afloat. It is these broader consequences that give the accountant's work meaning, not the actual number side of the work.

I recall a lady who was a cleaner in a school. She took great pride and satisfaction in her work because she provided a clean and healthy environment in which the students could learn and the teachers teach. This made her smile as she spoke of her work; she was content in her role.

It's useful to consider what the consequences might be if we weren't doing our roles. This might give you additional insight into the value of your work. Our work matters. We need to find a way to approach our work so that we take pride in it and so that we are doing the work for its own sake, not for the pay packet. We need to reshape our approach so that we are working for a reward that is internally meaningful, not for the external carrot of money. External motivation is short-lived and without depth of meaning. We can enjoy the state of flow in our work role, finding ourselves immersed in our day and content within ourselves.

CHAPTER 15
YOUR CREATIVE SELF

Why be creative? Why achieve a creative life?

Basically, we need to make things to know ourselves. By letting go and finding our creative side we can continue to express and discover who we are. We open up the inner world that is unique to us. There is a place of stillness and personal experience where all creative endeavour is born. We tap out of the world and into ourselves. Letting go and engaging with our creativity is also a wonderful way to find the joy of living. It can be fun to come up with something that is strange or different, or a creative answer to a daily problem. Creativity is the doorway into a richer and bigger world.

Being creative means connecting with our expressive skills, and externally communicating our internal subjective experiences. It is a window into ourselves and our uniqueness. It is not about the quality of what comes out, or someone else's subjective evaluation of what we produce. What contributes to our own well-being is the process and the expression of our unique selves.

Perfectionists usually lose the point here as they focus on jumping through hoops of performance expectations to meet their own excessively high standards or their concern for others' standards. It is in fact a wonderful exercise for a perfectionist to work on a sketch and then scrunch it up and throw it away. It is not the standard of what is produced that matters; it is the process of creating it that counts. The Tibetan monks have this down to a fine art. They create sand artwork, called 'sand mandalas', only to scoop up the sand at the end. The main point here is to demonstrate impermanence, but this ritual illustrates that the meaning of creativity is also fundamentally about the process, not the outcome.

We need to keep being creative each and every day. When people routinely tinker with building something in the back shed, or daily dabble with a sketch or craftwork or a garden design, they have the right idea. While we are all born with creative ability, we can become out of touch with our creative selves. We can work so hard, be so busy and focused on survival and obligation, that we can lose sight of that playful child that used to live in the world of imagination, dream, fantasy and creation. We need to dare to experience and live through our creative self again. Life can become boring, and play is the antidote. We need to listen to our inner voice.

> If we don't use our creative side, we do not lose it,
> we just misplace it for a while.

In the process of being creative we may sing a song, dance, sketch or paint a picture that expresses and represents how we are feeling. It is through our numerous avenues of creativity that we get in touch with our real self. For example, our homes are often an expression of our priorities, needs and value system. Whether the house is filled with animals, extremely tidy, very relaxed, or minimalistic to allow for spontaneous travel, our home is an expression of ourselves, and an avenue to further explore our creative voice.

Creativity is a formidable force. Through creativity comes expansion. There is no challenge that is beyond the human creative capacity. We have the capacity to create and to invent. We use our imagination to come up with solutions. This can apply to almost every field: environmental recovery, engineering, science, psychology, teaching, economic management. We are tapping into our incredibly strong creative impulse when, through invention, we solve the world's problems.

As artists will tell you, it is important to have freedom and independence in the expression of your craft in order to remain true to yourself. If you can do this, then huge credit to you. It is so exciting to be inspired by a new creative idea. Finding new avenues of creativity keeps many people vibrant and constantly expanding.

A warning, however: it takes practice to master an art form. You need to not only stick with it but *enjoy* the process of learning and refining. At first, you'll start with a gap between your aspirations and your skill level. For months – even years – you'll make stuff that's not that good. You might feel disappointment because you have aspirations and good taste, but you're not skilled yet. But most people who produce amazing creative work took years to refine their skill. Just because there is an enormous gap between what you can produce and your creative aspirations, this is not a reason to be discouraged; it is an invitation to enjoy the learning process. It is a path of creative growth to enjoy. It is only through time, practice and patience that your work will become as good as your ambitions.

Creativity is about having choice. It's a fork in the road. Through creativity, we realise that we have a multitude of possibilities and expressions of ourselves. You have the freedom to explore different parts of you that are not part of your daily norm. You are expanding. While on the whole there is consistency in your expression of yourself, you can be playful and open to new experiences. Don't think that you're 'all grown up now' or 'too old', or that you have to become fixed; we *always* need to be playful in our outlook. We are never too old. My dearest friend is eighty-one years old, but she lives with vibrancy, mischievousness and curiosity that would put most of us to shame. Age is not a factor to growth and expansion. Never go easy on yourself; we are never too old to keep reaching for our passions, our delights and our creativity through our curiosities.

Actually, creativity is an important tool for mastering aging. New projects, activities and adventures come from our creativity. I have a lovely eighty-three-year-old client who has just lost the love of his life. They were life companions, and he cared for her intensively during her last ten years of life. He of course fell into a dark grieving state after she died, and felt age come upon him. While we worked through his grief, I saw that his healing and regrowth really began when (with his permission) I asked his children to give him all of their 'fixer-upper' projects, a past passion of his. He soon created new routines, purpose and meaning. He was busy tinkering in his back shed, enjoying the challenge, the sense of satisfaction and his ability to help his family. He found a drive to eat, sleep and talk with his loved ones because he was busy with and passionate about his hobby. I credit his courage to start a new adventure in his life.

Creativity can challenge rigidity. We need to resist setting ourselves into routines. We humans love patterns; they can help us streamline our life. But we often hide behind them, scared of new things. Routines can help us feel familiar, secure and in control. Without some flexibility and spontaneity, even pleasures can become routine. We habituate to what we used to find fun, and our 'fun' routine can become a chore. As long as we have an injection of novelty in conversation, circumstance and challenges, then we are fine.

We might unsettle and perplex our loved ones when we broaden ourselves. Changes in us may create shock and not be popular. Our loved ones may have a lot invested in us being consistent. That is okay; we can be sensitive to their fear of the unfamiliar. When someone gets divorced, for example, their family and friends might react negatively because their own world has been changed as a result. They are not looking at the significant need for the divorce. They are predominantly looking through their own lens and their own needs. Another example is when we change our role. We may have played the role of caring and providing for others for much of our lives, and our family may disapprove as we expand our world to incorporate more self-expression and a healthier balance of living for ourselves.

The process of broadening ourselves is not, by the way, some hedonistic, self-indulgent spree. It is not the 'mid-life crisis' of 'out with the old and in with the new' in a desperate bid to avoid the reality of stages of development. It is actually the opposite. It is embracing where we are, who we are, and extending, growing and experimenting with other interests, passions and parts of ourselves. We need to value our healthy and meaningful relationships as they are ultimately what matters and they give us connection to others. We are actually enriching our relationships with others as we become more vibrant and appreciative within ourselves.

We need to write down ideas because they are precious and they will slip away. We need to notice our intuitions, and our piqued curiosities – the unconscious ingredients that get an airing through our dreams. I am forever noting down my creative thoughts – slips of paper cover a corner of my desk – and regularly add to my phone notebook. I don't want to lose the information and ideas that flow out of my mind. That is how this book is being written. Largely my subconscious is working on it, and keeps tapping me on the shoulder, saying, 'Hey, include this', or 'This is important', or 'How about you conceptualise it this way ...'. I dutifully record and appreciate.

Our creativity largely comes from our subconscious, which is an amazing and usually untapped resource, rich with ideas and information. If you leave your problems to percolate, you'll be amazed what the subconscious can come up with. It will add another layer of perspective.

We need to practise loosening the fibres of our imagination. After going to university for four years of undergraduate study, I found myself during my postgraduate university course being out of touch with my creativity. My role had changed from needing to learn and regurgitate information in undergrad, to needing to think more independently and creatively in postgrad. This was a problem. I had to rediscover and loosen up my creative independent thought again. I had to clean out those cobwebs. But my more independent and creative reasoning was sitting there, patiently waiting for me to crank it up again.

My creativity sprang back like an elastic band. It took time and it took effort as I encouraged myself to think independently, creatively and critically again. Doing post-graduate studies does help because suddenly you are 'let out' to decide your curious path, to create your argument, and to contribute a unique line of academic enquiry. This reconnection with our creativity is like changing gears, but the creative muscle is there within us; we just have to reach in and grab that part of us and start flexing it.

CHAPTER 16
PROVE SELF TO SELF – MEANING THROUGH HARD WORK

Half of the equation of state of flow is being in the zone where we are pushing ourselves and extending ourselves. This is great because we can only *really* enjoy that which we acquire through hard work and toil. The harder you work for something, the more you enjoy it. If something is easy, how much reward is there? When we push hard and achieve, we are better for it. We are better for what we have asked of ourselves.

If you want a castle, you need to build it, starting with the foundation. In pursuits that matter, while we can find ourselves in a state of flow, there is also a lot of behind-the-scenes, unglamorous hard work and dedication. Developing the skill of kicking yourself in the arse, as discussed in Book 6, Chapter 11, will help. True confidence within ourselves is achieved through pushing and extending ourselves and finding out what we are made of and capable of.

In contrast, there has been a move towards entitlement and victim behaviour in today's Western culture, which leaves individuals in a constant state of dissatisfaction and deep insecurity (see Book 6, Chapter 12). Our culture breeds rampant anxiety and depression because our sense of achievement and connection is lost. We are not building strong foundations. Rather than relying on hard work and perseverance, we have a habit of looking for shortcuts and quick fixes, which are complete illusions. The number of clients who state that they want a career or a point of achievement but then say in the next breath that they don't want to put the work in is remarkable. They express a real sense of 'poor me' and a victim mentality.

Such entitlement ignores basic cause and effect. If you want it, build it. If you don't build it, you can't have it. If you need to learn to apply yourself to build it, then start there. But it starts with *you*, not with the world owing you any favours. Harsh but true.

CHAPTER 17
YOUR BODY: UNTAPPED RESOURCE FOR STATE OF FLOW

We understand the importance of health and fitness, but how many of us understand that we can use our body to harness our state of flow?

Our body has almost unlimited potential for enjoyment, and yet we do not harness this resource anywhere near full capacity. Few of us know the sheer joy of pushing ourselves to achieve a physical goal, like running a distance, or dancing beautifully, or climbing higher than before. If we choose our interest area, and we then work to keep extending in that strength, we can feel immense satisfaction and accomplishment and often a state of flow. We do not have to be elite athletes; we just have to take where we are now and then work to be a little stronger or a little faster. If our activity becomes boring as we have met our goals, we need to raise the stakes and set more goals. We need to find ways to measure our progress and create opportunities.

The use of our body does not just relate to strength and endurance, but also to refining our skills of using our senses. We can refine our sense of smell and our taste palate to wines and foods, for example. We can refine our skill of music appreciation, across many different music genres. We can increase our appreciation of art and beauty by again refining our tastes, knowledge and experiences. We can do all of this by just getting involved in clubs, classes or conversations, taking part in these new experiences, creating a reference point to hone our senses and build our unique perspective.

It is our conscious awareness of these motor and sensory skills that creates our state of flow. It is not the body alone, but our concentration and attention on these experiences. It is through our motivation, our thinking and our emotions that we are able to learn the discipline needed to hone these skills and enjoy the experience. Through our motor and sensory skills, we can tap into an almost unlimited amount of enjoyment, but only if we work to develop the required skills. Otherwise our body idles through life, not experiencing its physical potential or the subtle flavours of life that are there to be savoured. When we increase our skills of using our body and our senses, we can experience a whole other dimension to life. If we do not skill up our body and our senses, we miss opportunities and the richness of life around us.

CHAPTER 18
SELF-CONTAINED GOALS: DISSOLVE ANXIETY AND BOREDOM

To truly live well, we need to learn the art of having **self-contained goals**. I will explain, but let me give you a teaser: this means the ability to *find enjoyment in your difficult times*, to have inner harmony, to rarely get anxious or bored, and to routinely be in a state of flow. This is called being **autotelic**, or having an **autotelic self**. It is a remarkable skill to turn our tough times into opportunities for action or enjoyment.

The difference between someone who experiences a situation as an overwhelming threat and someone who can find enjoyment in it and see it as a strengthening opportunity is to do with the decision about *how to interpret and approach the situation*. The good news is that wealth, health and position have nothing to do with one's capacity to function with self-contained goals. This is to do with our control of our consciousness.

Translating potential threats into enjoyable challenges is a skill that can be learnt. Through this control of our consciousness, we can maintain inner harmony. This approach involves taking ownership of our experience and deciding to create our own primary goals in a situation, through consciously evaluating the situation. We choose how to approach a situation so that we can grow from it and make the most of it, rather than letting external forces shape our experience. When we do this, we are involved in what is going on around us. We are internally driven; we are buffered from boredom and anxiety, and importantly we reshape our situations to experience a state of flow on a regular basis.

An example is if we are overwhelmed by bills. Instead of experiencing this as a negative stress that makes us feel sorry for ourselves, we see it as a challenge to get creative, show our discipline, skill up and experience great satisfaction when we eventually get back into the black. After this chapter of financial challenge in our lives, we are genuinely in a more solid and experienced position for our future. We have learnt a lot, and we are more motivated and informed to take charge, so that in future our spending does not outweigh our earnings.

Another example is when we experience a physical injury. We can sit and lick our wound, or we can see it as a time to really learn about bolstering our holistic health. We learn to take charge of our body with our food intake, our sensible sleep habits, our rehabilitation and our future exercise. We now have a solid reason for making ongoing decisions about self-care.

Or at work, we might decide to take a crisis on as a challenge and stay close to our inner selves as we coach ourselves through with supportive and encouraging self-talk. Once we are through our tough times, we have learnt so much; we are stronger.

We may be in a car accident. This is a time to take pride in being sensible in how we solve problems, getting through the immediate dangers and then focusing on the next stage of recovery and getting back on track. We can only optimally recover from any trauma if we are compassionate towards ourselves. It is natural to feel fear following danger. This self-compassion is a mindful choice. The key is to grab your challenging situation and take charge of it. You do not get dragged along; you choose to pick it up and shape the situation to get your desired outcome. And well done to you, as you become bold and navigate your approach.

How do we do this? How do we transform our situations and become internally driven? First of all, we learn to appraise the situation and create clear goals to strive for. We become increasingly practised and confident at making these decisions and choices. From big life-direction choices to mundane daily choices, we weigh up the situation, gathering and assessing the relevant information to help us decide our course.

Over time we can do this with increasing confidence and minimal fuss. With these choices, we pragmatically break down the pathway needed. What are our obstacles and our challenges? What are our resources? What is our strategy and the sequence of sub-goals we will need to meet? What skills do we need to learn? We monitor our progress and adjust our approach with an openness and adaptability to the feedback. If we are not learning from what is going well or not going well, we won't be able to optimise our approach, continue to skill up and achieve our goals effectively.

When choosing our own goals rather than letting an outside force choose our goals, we are more strongly dedicated to our course. This is of course a major positive and in itself brings power of conviction and a sense of ownership. When we feel internal control, our efforts are more reliable and consistent. We become more immersed and involved in our task. Being the captain of our own ship also means we have more control over steering it and adjusting our course if we feel we need to modify our approach or our end goal. This flexibility complements the consistency in efforts that we can bring to our project.

We need to avoid unrealistic goals, as well as the danger of just staying in the safe zone of our routines, where we do not have growth. We need to match our true capacity for growth with the demands and be realistic about our potential to reach our goal. There is also of course a direct marriage between our goals and the effort that we need to put in. The goals and the effort ultimately justify each other.

We must also sustain our attention so we can stay our course. By this I mean not only attention to the task that we are applying ourselves to, but attention to our consciousness *in that moment*. How are we going with our self-talk? Are we tired and therefore becoming less buoyant, less our engaged self? Then take a break, get some rest. Are we making the most of the situation by looking for pleasure in that moment, either by finding beauty in the moment, or finding satisfaction in learning or achieving, or just enjoying the moment to sit and relax?

This area taps enormously into the skill of mindfulness in the moment. Recall in Chapter 8 of this book when we talked about finding pleasure in the mundane (like cleaning kitty litter). There is significant overlap here, in that our capacity to reach our goals often involves creatively finding pleasure in a stressful or unpleasant situation.

The take-home message is that when we have control of our consciousness, if we focus on achieving solutions no matter how hard or long the road, we can create and find enjoyment in most challenges. The control of your consciousness that is required here demands self-awareness and determination. This is a disciplined mind. We are extending our achievements, our creativity and our personal capacity. We are always growing and being mindful.

To find meaning in life we need to have an overarching direction for our goals and our value system. What are we working towards? What expression of ourselves are we nurturing? What matters in our lives that keeps guiding our choices? This sense of direction – this constant purpose in our goals – gives us a sense of harmony. It is a nod to guiding our lives towards that authentic expression of ourselves. When we understand how flow works and live through this approach instead of wasting our time on boredom or anxiety, we can actually grow our energy. This is optimal experience.

IN CONCLUSION

Reflect: is your life too boring, too stressful, too lacking in passion? Are you living as if your life is a conveyor belt – day in, day out, minimal pleasure, just on repeat? If so, I implore you to take seriously your task of creating meaning in your life and diving into a state of flow. Make it your priority to find windows in which you create purpose and joy, either in approaching the mundane with intent to find pleasure, or in relishing an area of play, creativity or learning. I'm excited for you. Prepare for a sharp climb in your passion and pleasure in life.

FURTHER READING

I would like to acknowledge the wisdom of other authors and philosophers whose insights I have shared in this series. If you'd like to know more about 'flow', I recommend the works of Mihaly Csikszentmihalyi, whose findings I have referred to in this book. They are:

Csikszentmihalyi, M (1998), *Finding flow: the psychology of engagement with everyday life.* Little Brown, New York.

Csikszentmihalyi, M (2008), *Flow: the psychology of optimal experience.* HarperCollins Publishers, New York.

The works of Jon Kabat-Zinn will also help deepen your understanding of concepts in this book:

Kabat-Zinn, J (2006), *Coming to our senses: healing ourselves and the world through mindfulness.* Hyperion, New York.

Kabat-Zinn, J (2011), *Wherever you go, there you are.* Hyperion, New York.

And, finally, if you wish to explore the topics I have touched on briefly in this book more deeply, you might like to try the other books in the 'Signposts for Living' series by Dr Kirsten Hunter:

Book 1: Control your Consciousness – In the Driver's Seat

Book 2: Understanding Myself – Be an Expert

Book 4: Understanding Others – Loved Ones to Tricky Ones

Book 5: Parenting – Love, Pride, Apprenticeship

Book 6: Nailing Being an Adult – Have the Skills

ACKNOWLEDGEMENTS

To Jon, my beautiful husband, your support is constant. I can always rely on you to be in my corner, patiently championing me on while I sit typing away. With writing, having someone who believes in you makes all the difference. Thank you that it is always 'us' facing the next challenge, the next hurdle. I love you.

My devoted mum has been the rock through my childhood and every chapter of my adulthood. No child could have a more extraordinary mum. I'm proud of you and I love you.

Our five boys, Lachlan, James, Tobias, Jack, and George, when you heard that your mum was writing books, non-fiction and fiction, your response was simply 'of course she is'. When you heard mum was publishing, your response was 'of course she is'. When we talk about the book being successful in reaching a wide audience, your response, 'of course it will'. You boys are so beautiful. Ever-resounding support, thank you. I love you.

Vanya Lowther, you are the smartest person I know, and perhaps the wisest. You are also my closest and my lifelong friend. Thank you for taking on the mammoth task of being the first person to put your eyes on the *Signposts for Living* books. Your perseverance, your contribution and brainpower was and is so appreciated. I love you.

Jane Smith, I agree with Stephen King, 'to write is human, to edit is divine'. Thank you for your eye for detail, your grammatical wizardry and staying fresh when there was so much work to do. You're a talented gem.

ABOUT THE AUTHOR

Dr Kirsten Hunter is a clinical psychologist with 20 years' experience working with children, adolescents, adults, and couples across the expanse of clinical areas. Between running her private practice, enjoying time with her family, and writing her books, Kirsten juggles a range of passions – particularly for scuba diving and hiking. Kirsten is known for diving deep into life, creating and embracing all of life's opportunities. Born in Brisbane, she now lives in Toowoomba, Australia, with her six men: her husband and their five sons. Even their pets are male ...

www.ingramcontent.com/pod-product-compliance
Lightning Source LLC
Chambersburg PA
CBHW041958080526
44588CB00021B/2794